A BUSINESS APPROACH TO MARIJUANA FARMING

Complete Entrepreneurial Step By Step Guide To Marijuana Garden From Scratch

ZHURI HART

DISCLAIMER

This book is intended to provide general information and insights on adopting a business approach to farming. The content within is based on the author's knowledge and experiences up to the date of publication. It is essential to recognize that the field of agriculture is dynamic, influenced by various factors such as market conditions, climate, and regulatory changes.

Readers are advised to conduct thorough research, seek professional advice, and consider their unique circumstances before implementing any strategies or practices discussed in this book. The author and publisher disclaim any responsibility for the accuracy, completeness, or suitability of the information provided. The book is not a substitute for professional advice, and the author and publisher shall not be liable for any damages or losses arising from the use or reliance on the information presented herein.

Individual results may vary, and success in farming enterprises is contingent upon numerous variables. The author encourages readers to consult with relevant experts, agricultural extension services, and legal or financial professionals to tailor strategies to their specific needs and local conditions.

This book is not intended to be a comprehensive guide to all aspects of farming, and readers should exercise their judgment and discretion in applying the principles discussed. The author and publisher do not endorse any specific products, services, or companies mentioned in this book unless explicitly stated.

By reading this book, the reader acknowledges and accepts the inherent uncertainties in agricultural endeavors and agrees to use the information at their own risk.

TABLE OF CONTENTS

ABOUT THE BOOK

"A Business Approach to Marijuana Farming" is a thorough manual created to give farmers, business owners, and marijuana aficionados the information and resources they need to successfully navigate the challenging terrain of marijuana growing and take advantage of the sector's expanding prospects. The book explores many aspects of marijuana growing and offers insightful information about the environment, methods of cultivation, business planning, operations, legal issues, and potential future developments in the field.

Setting the scene, the book provides a summary of the marijuana market, emphasizing current trends, future development potential, and the regulatory landscape. Readers must possess this fundamental knowledge to comprehend the framework within which they will be working. It offer comprehensive guidance, beginning with the necessities of beginning a marijuana farm, such as choosing a strain, obtaining a license, choosing a location, and adhering to regulations.

The book's examination of cultivation methods, which distinguishes between indoor and outdoor cultivation, and its thorough coverage of important elements including soil management, lighting systems, and insect control are among its strong points. This useful information guarantees that readers will be well-prepared to choose their gardening techniques.

The planning, operations, and management chapters, which are business-focused, provide a comprehensive strategy for managing a profitable marijuana cultivation firm. Through highlighting the significance of formulating a business strategy, accounting for finances, advertising tactics, and daily management, the book offers readers a thorough road map for starting and maintaining a successful company in the cannabis sector.

The thorough examination of legal and regulatory issues, which takes into account the cannabis industry's constant change, is a noteworthy aspect. To ensure that readers are adequately equipped to manage the intricate legal environment surrounding marijuana farming, this section addresses a variety of themes, including risk mitigation, taxation considerations, regulatory compliance, and legal issues.

In addition, the book provides insight into upcoming developments and trends in the sector, including research and development, market evolution, innovative technologies, and international opportunities. With this forward-looking viewpoint, readers can remain on top of developments and set themselves up for success in a field that is still changing quickly.

"A Business Approach to Marijuana Farming" is an invaluable tool for anyone looking to get started in the marijuana market or grow their business.

CHAPTER ONE

MARIJUANA FARMING INTRODUCTION

BACKGROUND

Before diving into any conversation, it is necessary to lay out the background. The background offers the theoretical, social, or historical context necessary to comprehend the topic at hand.

The background acts as a road map for readers in a variety of situations, taking them through the development or introduction of a specific subject. It provides a historical viewpoint, but it also illuminates the forces and influences that have influenced the topic over time.

Within the larger context of scholarly or professional writing, the background section frequently clarifies the importance of the selected subject. It contributes to the response to the basic question "why?" by highlighting the subject's importance and relevance within a specific industry or field of study. By bridging the gap between the past and the present, this section establishes the foundation for a thorough comprehension of the material that follows.

LEGAL ASPECTS TO TAKE INTO ACCOUNT

Legal issues are integral to many disciplines and sectors, significantly influencing the environment in which decisions are made, carried out, and operated. In every field—business, technology, healthcare, or otherwise—the legal system is a vital component that establishes the limits and conditions that govern the activities of people and organizations.

Examining laws, rules, and court rulings that impact and regulate a certain topic is necessary to comprehend legal considerations.

It entails analyzing the rights, obligations, and responsibilities that stakeholders must manage about the law. This complex dimension interacts with social, ethical, and economic factors to create a framework that aims to maintain justice and fairness while balancing conflicting interests.

International treaties, conventions, and agreements are frequently taken into account in the dynamic and always-changing legal landscape. Because of the global nature of today's society, it is important to understand how legal ideas affect people and organizations on a transnational level, despite boundaries.

Furthermore, legal issues are essential to proactive planning and risk management rather than being limited to reactive actions. For example, to maintain a viable and compliant operation, businesses need to handle intellectual property laws, contract negotiations, and employment requirements. Similar to this, technical developments have a wide range of legal ramifications, including disputes over intellectual property rights and issues with data protection and privacy.

The domain of legal issues is complex and wide-ranging, permeating both professional and societal landscapes. It is a crucial component of ethical behavior, governance, and decision-making that affects how people, groups, and society as a whole behave. Upon navigating the complex interaction of legal principles, it is clear that having a sophisticated understanding of these factors is not only legally necessary but also strategically essential.

CHAPTER TWO

THE SITUATION OF THE CANNABIS INDUSTRY

AN OVERVIEW OF THE CANNABIS MARKET

In recent years, the marijuana industry has transformed itself, emerging from the shadows of illegality to become a rapidly growing and legal market. With the changing legal and sociological perceptions of cannabis, the market has become more complex, offering a wide range of opportunities as well as difficulties.

The marijuana business is divided into several sectors, including retail, processing, distribution, and growing. The two main species of the plant, Cannabis sativa and Cannabis indicia, are used to make a variety of items, including hemp-derived products like CBD and medical and recreational marijuana. The industry is expanding because of the growing recognition of cannabis's medicinal benefits as well as its potential economic impact and shifting views toward the drug.

GROWTH AND TRENDS IN THE MARKET

The marijuana industry is subject to dynamic market trends that are shaped by various variables, including changing customer tastes, technology breakthroughs, and regulatory developments. Growing consumer demand for marijuana for medical and recreational purposes has prompted higher spending on R&D, new product development, and market growth. Consolidation and strategic alliances are growing more frequent as the sector develops, which makes the market more complex and competitive.

ENVIRONMENT REGULATION

The legal framework, which differs greatly between states, also influences how the marijuana business expands. Certain areas have accepted legalization for both medical and recreational purposes, creating a flourishing market with clear laws. Others uphold stringent bans, which creates a more covert and illegal industry.

Keeping up with legislative changes is essential for industry participants, as it presents hurdles for organizations looking to operate legally and ethically in this complicated regulatory context.

OPPORTUNITIES AND CHALLENGES

Opportunities-wise, the marijuana business offers a variety of options for investors, job seekers, and entrepreneurs. Innovation is facilitated by the market's expansion, which might lead to the creation of novel strains with particular therapeutic qualities or novel ways to consume them. Within the marijuana ecosystem, ancillary businesses like packaging, marketing services, and technology solutions can also prosper.

The marijuana business is not without its difficulties, though. The industry's expansion may be impeded by financial constraints, regulatory concerns, and the persistent stigma around cannabis. Furthermore, concerns about product standardization, quality assurance, and sustainable practices need to be continuously addressed. It can be challenging to strike a balance between profitable operations and ethical business practices, particularly in a sector that is still undergoing fast change.

The landscape of the marijuana market is dynamic, characterized by changes in regulations, public views, and technical improvements. Businesses and stakeholders must handle the opportunities and difficulties present in this dynamic industry as the market trends upward. The path ahead most likely entails ongoing regulatory framework adaption, creative product development, and a dedication to ethical and sustainable business practices.

CHAPTER THREE

HOW TO BEGIN GROWING MARIJUANA

SELECTING THE PROPER STRAIN

Choosing the right strain of marijuana is an important choice that will have a big effect on how successful your growing endeavor is. Distinct strains exhibit unique traits like as growth patterns, profiles of cannabinoids, and resilience against pests and illnesses. When making this choice, factors including soil type, climate, and resource availability should be taken into account. Furthermore, knowing the demand on the market for particular strains will assist direct your choice, guaranteeing a more lucrative and long-lasting cultivation.

PERMITS AND LICENSES

Since local laws vary greatly, marijuana farmers must understand the legal environment. One of the most important steps in ensuring compliance with local, state, and federal laws is obtaining the required licenses and permits. This procedure necessitates in-depth investigation and comprehension of your jurisdiction's regulatory standards. The licensing procedure can be streamlined by interacting with local authorities, going to workshops, and hiring legal advice. This will lay a strong basis for a legal and prosperous marijuana cultivation business.

INFRASTRUCTURE AND SITE SELECTION

The success of your marijuana farm as a whole is greatly influenced by its location. Conditions including soil type, climate, and accessibility to water supplies need to be properly taken into account. A comprehensive site analysis will help you find possibilities and challenges that are specific to your area of choice. It is also crucial to invest in appropriate infrastructure, such as security measures, irrigation systems, and cost-effective energy sources. The infrastructure of the farm should be developed and planned appropriately to ensure long-term sustainability and operational effectiveness.

TECHNOLOGY AND EQUIPMENT

Investing in the correct equipment and embracing current technology can greatly increase your marijuana farm's output and efficiency. Keeping up with technology innovations is essential for everything from automatic irrigation systems to cutting-edge lighting solutions. Optimizing resource consumption and maximizing yields can be achieved by customizing your equipment choices to the unique requirements of your selected strain and the site's climatic circumstances. Updating and maintaining your equipment regularly keeps it dependable and facilitates a profitable and efficient growing process.

ADHERENCE TO THE STANDARDS

In the cannabis industry, following legal and industry requirements is a must. This covers a broad range of factors, such as product testing, labeling regulations, and growth techniques. Maintaining a respectable and legal organization requires being up to date on changing standards and best practices. Establishing a commitment to compliance and building trust with both regulatory bodies and consumers can be facilitated by putting quality control systems into place, documenting processes, and being involved in industry groups. You can further guarantee that your marijuana farm continuously meets and surpasses the set criteria in the developing cannabis business by conducting routine audits and self-evaluations.

CHAPTER FOUR

METHODS OF CULTIVATION

COMPARING INDOOR AND OUTDOOR CULTIVATION

The decision to cultivate indoors or outdoors has a significant impact on the overall success of a growing project. Growers can precisely control the temperature, humidity, and light cycles in an environment that is well-regulated when they cultivate inside. Year-round cultivation and the customization of growing conditions to meet the needs of individual plants are made possible by this degree of control. Conversely, outdoor cultivation is contingent upon ambient light levels and natural sunlight, which may lead to seasonal constraints but may also save operating expenses. Every technique has benefits and drawbacks, and the choice is frequently influenced by elements including temperature, available space, and the particular needs of the plants being grown.

THE GROWING MEDIUM AND SOIL

For cultivation to be successful, choosing the right soil or growing medium is essential. Important elements that affect plant growth are the pH, nutritional content, and makeup of the soil. Farmers frequently choose soil that drains properly and has a balanced nutritional profile. Furthermore, organic matter and compost are examples of soil additives that can improve soil fertility and structure. Growers employ alternate media like coco coir, perlite, or vermiculite in hydroponic or soilless production. Aeration, fertilizer delivery, water retention, and the particular needs of the farmed plants all play a role in the decision between soil and soilless media.

NUTRIENTS AND WATERING

A successful crop requires proper nitrogen management and irrigation. Careful observation is required of the kind and concentration of nutrients, as well as the frequency and volume of water. Plant health can be impacted by either under watering or overwatering, which can cause root issues. Plants need a balanced supply of micronutrients (such as iron, zinc, and copper) and macronutrients (like nitrogen, phosphorus, and potassium). Growers can use a variety of fertilizing techniques, such as synthetic or organic fertilizers, based on the growing system and the particular requirements of the plants.

SYSTEMS OF LIGHTING

Plant growth and development depend heavily on lighting, especially when growing plants indoors where natural sunshine may be scarce. Diverse lighting systems, including Light-Emitting Diodes (LEDs), fluorescent lights, and High-Intensity Discharge (HID) lamps, provide different intensities and spectrums. The energy efficiency of the lighting system, the amount of heat it produces, and the particular light needs of the plants being grown all play a role in the selection. To replicate natural daylight conditions and regulate the vegetative and flowering stages of plant growth, timed light cycles are frequently used.

CONTROLLING INSECTS AND ILLNESSES

Safeguarding crops and guaranteeing a good harvest depends on efficient pest and disease control. Biological controls, targeted pesticide application when needed, and preventive measures are all part of integrated pest management (IPM) programs. The introduction of beneficial insects, appropriate sanitation procedures, and routine plant monitoring are essential elements of integrated pest management (IPM). To avoid and handle pest and disease challenges, cultivators need to be proactive in identifying potential risks and putting appropriate safeguards in place. This will minimize the impact on the ecosystem as a whole and reduce the reliance on chemical interventions.

CHAPTER FIVE

PLANNING A BUSINESS

CREATING A BUSINESS STRATEGY

Any entrepreneur or business owner hoping to launch a profitable firm must first create a thorough business strategy. It acts as a road map outlining the objectives, approaches, and methods required for the company to succeed in the cutthroat industry. A well-written business plan helps with capital acquisition, investor attraction, and day-to-day operations guidance in addition to offering a clear vision for the future. The procedure entails carrying out a comprehensive market analysis, identifying the target market, summarizing the business's distinct value offer, and creating a growth strategy.

ASPECTS OF FINANCE

A company plan must include financial considerations, which include budgeting, revenue predictions, and funding sources, among other things. A strong financial plan guarantees the company's long-term viability and profitability.

It entails a careful analysis of the initial outlay, ongoing costs, and projected income. Determining the break-even point and developing financial predictions that provide information about the success of the business going forward are other financial issues. Businesses can make decisions that contribute to long-term success by thoroughly examining these elements.

SETTING A BUDGET

Financial planning is not complete without budgeting, which entails assigning resources to various business divisions. It gives a thorough picture of projected costs and revenue, assisting companies in efficiently allocating their financial resources. A well-organized budget takes human salaries, marketing costs, operational costs, and other overheads into account. Businesses can monitor and manage their expenditure, prevent needless financial hardship, and make required strategic modifications by creating a realistic budget.

ESTIMATES OF REVENUE

A revenue projection is a forecast that shows how much money a company anticipates making over a given time frame. It entails pricing plans, income stream identification, and sales forecasting. Businesses may evaluate their growth potential, set realistic financial targets, and allocate resources effectively with the help of accurate revenue estimates. When creating revenue predictions, it is critical to take competition data, industry trends, and customer demand into account to provide a comprehensive and realistic picture of the company's financial future.

SOURCES OF FUNDING

It is imperative for firms operating at different stages of development to identify and secure suitable funding sources. Knowing the funding choices that are accessible is crucial, whether you're hoping to grow your business or just need the first launch funds. Conventional bank financing, government grants, angel investors, venture capital, and crowd sourcing are examples of possible sources. Every source has pros and cons of its own, and a well-researched business plan should provide a customized strategy for securing and overseeing the capital required for long-term expansion.

PROMOTION AND LABELING:

Important components of a business strategy that help build a strong brand and draw clients are marketing and branding. A clearly defined marketing strategy describes how a company plans to market its goods and services, connect with its target market, and set itself apart from rivals. The goal of branding initiatives is to create a distinct and identifiable identity that appeals to consumers. Effective marketing and branding techniques help businesses develop their brand equity, cultivate client loyalty, and eventually boost revenue growth.

RISK CONTROL

The proactive process of recognizing, evaluating, and reducing possible risks and obstacles that could influence a company's performance is known as risk management. A thorough risk management plan in a business plan includes identifying external and internal risks, creating backup plans, and putting precautions in place to lessen unfavorable effects. These might include shifts in the market, advancements in technology, adherence to regulations, and hazards associated with operations. Businesses may improve their resilience and adaptability and ensure a more stable and secure future by proactively addressing possible hazards.

A comprehensive business plan integrates these essential ideas to offer a strategic and all-encompassing framework for achievement. Every component, from risk management to marketing plans and financial concerns, is vital in assisting companies in achieving long-term sustainability and sustainable growth in a cutthroat marketplace.

CHAPTER SIX

THE MANAGEMENT AND OPERATIONS

REGULAR ACTIVITIES

A successful organization's daily operations, which include all of the regular jobs and activities needed to keep the business running smoothly, are its foundation. This involves doing everything from supervising staff work and managing daily workflows to making sure crucial procedures are carried out effectively. Regular operations require a sharp eye for detail because even small interruptions can have a domino effect on overall output. For businesses to achieve their goals and stay competitive, a well-organized and structured approach to daily operations is essential.

TRAINING AND STAFFING

A workforce's productivity and effectiveness are directly impacted by these two essential organizational management functions. Recruiting is just one aspect of strategic staffing; another is allocating resources according to duties and skill sets. Sufficient training is crucial for endowing workers with the requisite abilities and understanding, cultivating a capable and flexible group. Constant training program investment benefits the organization's overall growth and success as well as the professional development of the individual. An adequately staffed and trained workforce is better able to manage obstacles and constructively contribute to the goals of the organization.

Ensuring that products or services meet or surpass established standards requires quality control, which is an essential component. To track, assess, and improve output quality, it entails methodical processes and procedures. Ensuring brand reputation, fostering customer trust, and lowering the likelihood of errors or defects all depend on the implementation of strict quality control procedures. Businesses frequently use a variety of instruments and approaches, like Total Quality Management or Six Sigma, to preserve and raise the caliber of their goods and services. To handle new problems and make sure that quality requirements are constantly fulfilled, constant observation and adjustment are required.

RECORD-KEEPING AND COMPLIANCE

Ethical, lawful, and efficient business operations depend on efficient record-keeping and compliance management. Maintaining precise documentation guarantees openness, and responsibility, and eases the process of making decisions. Respecting the laws, rules, and industry standards that are pertinent to the operations of the organization is known as compliance. Strong record-keeping procedures and compliance guidelines are essential for reducing risks, averting legal problems, and upholding a positive company reputation.

Conducting routine audits and reviews is crucial for pinpointing areas that require enhancement and guaranteeing that the organization stays compliant with relevant regulations and guidelines.

ECOLOGICAL METHODS

Sustainability practices are becoming more and more important for businesses looking to strike a balance between financial success and social and environmental responsibility in today's global business environment. Resource efficiency, waste reduction, and social impact are just a few of the many facets that make up sustainable practices. Long-term viability and good corporate citizenship are facilitated by implementing environmentally friendly procedures, switching to renewable energy sources, and participating in community projects. Adopting a sustainable approach can result in cost savings, enhanced brand perception, and adaptability to shifting market conditions, in addition to being in line with societal norms. Businesses that include sustainable practices in their daily operations show that they care about a better, more conscientious future.

MARKETING AND DISTRIBUTION

Having a thorough understanding of market demand is essential to any sales and distribution plan that is going to be successful. A detailed examination of customer trends, behavior, and preferences is required for this. Businesses can detect new needs and predict changes in demand by utilizing market research techniques. With the help of this information, decisions can be made with knowledge and products can be customized to match the changing needs of the intended market. Comprehending market demand also aids in inventory optimization, reduces the possibility of overstock or stock outs, and eventually improves the overall effectiveness of the supply chain.

DISTRIBUTION CHANNELS

A key factor in linking products with end users is the effectiveness of the distribution channels. For products to reach customers quickly and affordably, businesses must carefully plan and oversee these channels. The choice relies on the characteristics of the product and the preferences of the target market, whether selling through direct channels like company-owned stores or online platforms, or indirect channels involving middlemen like wholesalers and retailers. Achieving maximum sales potential and optimal market coverage requires striking the correct balance between direct and indirect channels.

DEVELOPING PARTNERSHIPS WITH DISPENSARIES

Proper dispensary partnerships are crucial for efficient sales and distribution in sectors like wellness, health, and pharmaceuticals. These are relationships based on mutual benefit, trust, and dependability rather than just business dealings. Businesses can better understand the unique needs of the market and customize their offerings by working in tandem with dispensaries and maintaining consistent communication. Establishing a strong network of dependable dispensaries benefits suppliers and retailers alike by promoting effective product placement and enhancing brand credibility.

MARKETING STRATEGIES

Developing successful marketing plans is essential to raising sales and building brand recognition. Combining traditional and digital marketing strategies with audience-specific targeting is known as a holistic approach. To engage customers and develop a devoted clientele, businesses can make use of influencer partnerships, content marketing, and social media platforms. In a crowded market, differentiation is further enhanced by matching marketing initiatives with the distinctive value propositions of the products. Periodic assessments and adjustments of marketing strategies based on market feedback and performance metrics are essential for staying relevant and maintaining a competitive edge.

PRICING AND SALES TACTICS

Determining the right pricing strategy is a delicate balance between perceived value and market competitiveness. Businesses must consider factors such as production costs, competitor pricing, and consumer willingness to pay. Employing dynamic pricing models that adapt to market fluctuations can also be advantageous. Additionally, implementing effective sales tactics, such as bundling, discounts, or loyalty programs, can stimulate demand and incentivize customer loyalty. Regularly evaluating the effectiveness of pricing and sales tactics ensures adaptability to market changes and helps maintain a strategic advantage in a dynamic business environment.

CHAPTER SEVEN

NAVIGATING LEGAL AND REGULATORY CHALLENGES

STAYING COMPLIANT WITH EVOLVING REGULATIONS

Navigating legal and regulatory challenges in today's dynamic business environment requires a keen awareness of the constantly evolving landscape. Staying compliant with regulations is not just a matter of meeting current requirements but also anticipating and adapting to changes. Regularly monitoring and interpreting new laws and regulations at local, national, and international levels is crucial for businesses aiming to navigate these complexities successfully.

Companies must establish robust compliance programs that encompass a proactive approach to understanding regulatory updates. This involves not only legal teams but also collaboration with other departments to ensure a comprehensive understanding of how changes may impact various aspects of the business. Additionally, fostering a culture of compliance among employees is essential, as it enhances the organization's ability to identify and address potential issues before they escalate.

TAXATION CONSIDERATIONS

Taxation considerations are integral to a company's financial strategy and overall business planning. Understanding the tax implications of different business activities, structures, and transactions is essential for maintaining compliance and optimizing financial outcomes. Tax planning should be aligned with the organization's broader strategic goals, taking into account both domestic and international tax regulations.

Engaging with tax experts and professionals becomes crucial for businesses to navigate the complexities of tax codes and regulations. This collaboration aids in identifying opportunities for tax incentives, credits, and deductions, while simultaneously mitigating risks associated with potential liabilities. It's essential to stay informed about changes in tax laws, as they can significantly impact the financial health and sustainability of a business.

LEGAL ISSUES AND RISK MITIGATION

Legal issues are inherent in the business landscape, and understanding how to identify, manage, and mitigate these risks is vital for long-term success. Proactively addressing legal challenges involves a comprehensive risk management approach. This includes regularly conducting legal audits to assess compliance, contractual obligations, and potential liabilities.

Effective risk mitigation requires close collaboration between legal teams and other stakeholders within the organization. Developing clear and transparent contracts, implementing dispute resolution mechanisms, and staying informed about industry-specific legal trends are critical components of a robust risk management strategy.

Additionally, businesses should consider obtaining appropriate insurance coverage to protect against unforeseen legal challenges.

ADVOCACY AND INDUSTRY ASSOCIATIONS

Engaging with industry associations and advocacy groups is a strategic approach to navigating legal and regulatory challenges. Participation in these forums provides businesses with a platform to voice concerns, influence policy decisions, and stay informed about industry-specific developments. Advocacy efforts can extend to collaboration with other businesses to collectively address shared challenges and shape regulatory frameworks that support industry growth.

By actively participating in industry associations, businesses not only gain valuable insights into upcoming regulatory changes but also contribute to the formulation of policies that align with their interests.

CHAPTER EIGHT

FUTURE TRENDS AND INNOVATIONS

EMERGING TECHNOLOGIES

In the ever-evolving landscape of future trends and innovations, emerging technologies play a pivotal role in shaping the way industries operate and individuals interact. The convergence of artificial intelligence, block chain, quantum computing, and 5G has the potential to revolutionize various sectors.

Artificial intelligence, with its ability to analyze vast amounts of data and make real-time decisions, is poised to transform healthcare, finance, and manufacturing.

Block chain, known for its decentralized and secure nature, is likely to redefine the way we approach transactions and data integrity. Quantum computing, on the other hand, holds promise for solving complex problems that are currently beyond the capabilities of classical computers. As these technologies mature, their synergies are expected to unlock unprecedented possibilities, ushering in a new era of innovation and efficiency.

MARKET EVOLUTION

The market evolution in the context of future trends is marked by dynamic shifts driven by changing consumer behaviors, regulatory landscapes, and technological advancements. Traditional market structures are giving way to more agile and digitally driven ecosystems. E-commerce, fueled by advancements in logistics and payment systems, continues to disrupt traditional retail models. Moreover, the rise of the sharing economy, powered by platforms that facilitate peer-to-peer transactions, is reshaping industries such as transportation and accommodation.

The emphasis on sustainability and ethical business practices is influencing consumer preferences, leading to the emergence of eco-friendly products and services. In this evolving marketplace, companies that adapt swiftly to changing dynamics and embrace innovative business models are likely to thrive.

INTERNATIONAL OPPORTUNITIES

The global nature of future trends and innovations presents vast international opportunities for businesses willing to explore and expand beyond their borders. As technology breaks down geographical barriers, companies can tap into new markets and collaborations, fostering a more interconnected world. Cross-border partnerships in research and development, joint ventures, and strategic alliances can accelerate innovation by leveraging diverse expertise and resources.

The internationalization of supply chains and the advent of digital platforms facilitate seamless global transactions, allowing businesses to access a wider customer base. Emerging economies, with their increasing technological adoption rates, offer untapped markets for products and services.

To capitalize on international opportunities, organizations need to embrace cultural diversity, navigate regulatory landscapes, and employ adaptive strategies that resonate with diverse consumer preferences.

RESEARCH AND DEVELOPMENT

The engine driving future trends and innovations is undeniably research and development (R&D). Investing in R&D is crucial for staying ahead of the curve and maintaining a competitive edge. Continuous exploration of novel ideas, experimentation with cutting-edge technologies, and the pursuit of breakthrough innovations are central to R&D endeavors.

Government initiatives, private sector investments, and academic collaborations contribute to fostering a conducive environment for research. The integration of interdisciplinary approaches and the cross-pollination of ideas from various fields accelerate the development of groundbreaking solutions. As R&D initiatives progress, there is a growing emphasis on ethical considerations, sustainability, and responsible innovation. The outcomes of robust R&D efforts not only propel technological advancements but also shape the ethical frameworks that govern their deployment in society.